Candle Time

Las Posadas

Jennifer Blizin Gillis

Heinemann Library
Chicago, Illinois

© 2002 Reed Educational & Professional Publishing
Published by Heinemann Library,
an imprint of Reed Educational & Professional Publishing,
Chicago, Illinois

Customer Service 888-454-2279
Visit our website at www.heinemannlibrary.com

Designed by Sue Emerson, Heinemann Library; Page layout by Ginkgo Creative, Inc.
Printed and bound in the U.S.A. by Lake Book

06 05 04 03 02
10 9 8 7 6 5 4 3 2 1

Library of Congress Cataloging-in-Publication Data
Gillis, Jennifer, 1950-
   Las Posadas / Jennifer Blizin Gillis.
      p. cm. — (Candle time)
Includes index.
Summary: A basic introduction to the Las Posadas holiday.
   ISBN: 1-58810-531-8 (HC), ISBN 1-58810-740-X (Pbk.)
   1. Posadas (Social custom)—Juvenile literature. 2. Christmas—Mexico—Juvenile literature. [1. Posadas (Social
custom) 2. Christmas—Mexico. 3. Holidays. 4. Mexican-Americans—Social life and customs.] I. Title. II. Series.
GT4987.16 .G55 2002
394.266—dc21

2001004646

Acknowledgments
The author and publishers are grateful to the following for permission to reproduce copyright material:
pp. 4, 7, 8, 20, 22 Robert Frerck/Odyssey/Chicago; p. 5 Jerome Longawa; p. 9 TRIP/S. Grant; p. 10 Jose Carrillo/
PhotoPhile; p. 11 Doug Wilson; p. 12 Albert Molday/National Geographic Image Collection; p. 13 Danny Lehman/Corbis;
p. 14 Charles and Josette Lenars/Corbis; p. 15 Myrleen Ferguson Cate/PhotoEdit, Inc.; pp. 16, 21 Rafael Crisostomo;
p. 17 Robin Dunitz/DDB Stock Photo; p. 18 Gary A. Conner/DDB Stock Photo; p. 19 Spencer Grant/Photo Edit, Inc.

Cover photograph courtesy of Robert Frerck/Odyssey/Chicago

Every effort has been made to contact copyright holders of any material reproduced in this book. Any omissions will
be rectified in subsequent printings if notice is given to the publisher.

Special thanks to our advisory panel for their help in the preparation of this book:
Eileen Day, Preschool Teacher
Chicago, IL

Paula Fischer, K–1 Teacher
Indianapolis, IN

Sandra Gilbert,
Library Media Specialist
Houston, TX

Angela Leeper,
Educational Consultant
North Carolina Department
of Public Instruction
Raleigh, NC

Pam McDonald, Reading Teacher
Winter Springs, FL

Melinda Murphy,
Library Media Specialist
Houston, TX

Helen Rosenberg, MLS
Chicago, IL

Anna Marie Varakin,
Reading Instructor
Western Maryland College

Some words are shown in bold, **like this.**
You can find them in the picture glossary on page 23.
You say lahs po-SAH-dahs.

Contents

What Is Las Posadas?

Las Posadas is a candle time.

It is a Christmas celebration from Mexico.

It is for people who believe in **Jesus**.

They remember the night he was born.

When Do People Celebrate Las Posadas?

DECEMBER						
1	2	3	4	5	6	7
8	9	10	11	12	13	14
15	16	17	18	19	20	21
22	23	24	25	26	27	28
29	30	31				

Las Posadas is in December.

It lasts for nine nights.

The last night is called **Nochebuena.**

That is Spanish for Christmas Eve.

What Do People Do During Las Posadas?

People walk in a **procession**.

They pretend to look for a place to stay.

The procession stops at a house or church.

People sing a song and ask to come inside.

How Do People Dress for Las Posadas?

Some people dress like shepherds.

Some children dress like **angels**.

sombrero

Other people dress in Mexican clothes.

Some people wear big hats called **sombreros**.

What Lights Are There at Las Posadas?

farol

Some people carry lanterns.

They are called **faroles**.

farolito

People put candles in bags outside.

They are called **farolitos**.

What Do the Decorations Look Like?

There are special decorations inside the houses.

They are called **nacimientos**.

One decoration is the **manger**.

On Christmas Eve, people put
a statue of **Jesus** there.

What Foods Do People Eat for Las Posadas?

taco   enchiladas

People eat special Mexican foods.

There are **enchiladas** and tacos.

Some people drink juice.

Other people drink hot chocolate.

What Games Do People Play at Las Posadas?

Grown-ups hang a **piñata**.

At Las Posadas, it is a big paper star.

Children break open the piñata.

Candy and fruit fall out!

Are There Gifts for Las Posadas?

Children get candy and fruit from the **piñata**.

Sometimes grown-ups give children little bags.

The bags have toys and candy inside.

Quiz

What are these things called?

Look for the answers on page 24.

?

?   **?**

Picture Glossary

 **angel**
page 10

 **enchiladas**
(en-chee-LAH-das)
page 16

 **farol**
(fah-ROLL)
page 12

 **farolitos**
(fah-ro-LEE-toes)
page 13

 **Jesus**
pages 5, 15

 **manger**
(MAIN-jer)
page 15

 **nacimientos**
(nah-see-me-YEN-toes)
page 14

 **Nochebuena**
(NOH-chay-BWAYN-ah)
page 7

 **piñata**
(peen-YAH-ta)
pages 18, 19, 20

 **procession**
(pro-SEH-shun)
pages 8, 9

 **sombrero**
(sohm-BREH-ro)
page 11

Note to Parents and Teachers

Reading for information is an important part of a child's literacy development. Learning begins with a question about something. Help children think of themselves as investigators and researchers by encouraging their questions about the world around them. Each chapter in this book begins with a question. Read the question together. Look at the pictures. Talk about what you think the answer might be. Then read the text to find out if your predictions were correct. Think of other questions you could ask about the topic, and discuss where you might find the answers. Assist children in using the picture glossary and the index to practice new vocabulary and research skills.

Index

Answers to quiz on page 22

nacimiento

angel farol

24